INVISIBLE CHAINS

INVISIBLE CHAINS

Understanding how to break bondages and experience freedom

Demecia Lewis

XULON PRESS

Xulon Press
2301 Lucien Way #415
Maitland, FL 32751
407.339.4217
www.xulonpress.com

© 2017 by Demecia Lewis

All rights reserved solely by the author. The author guarantees all contents are original and do not infringe upon the legal rights of any other person or work. No part of this book may be reproduced in any form without the permission of the author. The views expressed in this book are not necessarily those of the publisher.

Unless otherwise indicated, Scripture quotations taken from the King James Version (KJV) – *public domain*.

Scripture quotations taken from the New King James Version. (NKJV). Copyright 1979, 1980, 1982 by Thomas Nelson, Inc. Used by permission. All rights reserved.

Scripture quotations taken from the New Living Translation copyright© (NLT) 1996, 2004, 2007 by Tyndale House Foundation.

Printed in the United States of America.

ISBN-13: 9781545615447

CONTENTS

FOREWORD BY **DR. LUIS LOPEZ JR** vii
ENDORSEMENTS xi
DEDICATION xv
PROLOGUE. xvii

One	The Wars in Life 3
Two	Time Ran from Me 17
Three	A New Wine Mentality 29
Four	A Fight for Your Mind. 41
Five	Was I Ever Going To Be Healed? 51
Six	The Man Who Saved Me. 65
Seven	Understanding Your Purpose. 77

EPILOGUE. 85
ACKNOWLEDGEMENTS 87
ABOUT THE AUTHOR. .91
APPENDIX A: PRAYER OF SALVATION
　　　　　　　AND THE BAPTISM OF
　　　　　　　THE HOLY SPIRIT. 93

FOREWORD

I HAVE READ MANY BOOKS. AND I WILL BE authentic to say that this book is an eye opener and a heart revealer because of the compassion and love of the author. Mrs. Demecia Lewis has poured her heart out into this book. And to be honest, I don't just say things just to say them, for those who know my wife (prophetess Michell Lopez) and I would know this to be true.

With much expectation, I stand believing that the Body of Jesus Christ would come to a place of brokenness and humility which would radiate off of our lives into the nostrils of the *Lord*, so He can see we are serious about Him, His people and His Glorious appearing. Stating this brings me to another point which is Love. The innumerable times the devil has tried so hard throughout the centuries to try to destroy us over and over again and could not. Yahshua/Jesus did say, the gates of hell will not prevail against the Church/us! Guess what? He was right! The power of God and His Love once again has prevailed. With no love, we have and are nothing no matter how great the gift.

Nevertheless, every single time our Adversary tries to mess with someone who does not get bound by any of the chains he brings, the devil is knocked down with a tremendous fall. This is what makes the enemy very angry. Demecia Lewis has expressed this very vividly and honestly. Therefore, as One Body, I know that the Church must rise up from any form of bondage in order to experience true freedom. A freedom only obtainable by Jesus the Messiah. Yes, I know many may not believe this statement, but regardless of the naysayers it still remains true to this day. This is one reason why it is so important to push through anything the son of perdition throws at you. Although the spirit of anti-christ is running rabid in our country and abroad, know for sure that God is still in control. He will not allow certain things to go on without any justice achieved or seen on earth. And anything that seems to hint any type of evil reign will fall and be judged and condemned. If not in this life, then in the life to come. King Jesus will *Prevail* and usher in tremendous triumphant justice to all. Like He said in His Word 3 times, "Vengeance is mine, I will repay." (Hebrews 10:30; Romans 12:19; Deuteronomy 32:35).

Many are not aware of the dangers of lust and other invisible chains. By God the Holy Spirit says, when a person saved or unsaved lusts after another person, demons look at you from that person's perspective and see you watching the individual in that manner and it gives them the right to come to you.

Foreword

And when it's time for you to be alone or at a sexual peak they entwine themselves with **your lust** as the book of James declares, and now you are found bound to that thing. In other words, we can adopt other spirits from other people by lusting after that person. These demons are watching you! So dangerous! We must be careful!

I hope this book alongside the Bible will help you take into consideration that God wants the best for you and so does Mrs. Demecia Lewis; as she has poured out her heart in this book. Demecia and her husband are an amazing couple. God bless you Reader and, I pray nothing but the best for you. Be blessed as you read this amazing book. Remember: You will accomplish!

—DR. LUIS LOPEZ JR (D.DIV.)
Best-selling author of 'The Counterfeit Christian'
Founder & CEO
LUIS LOPEZ MINISTRIES INTERNATIONAL
CHARLOTTE, NC

ENDORSEMENTS

As I write these lines, I thank God for being one angel short when He joined me with the love of my life, and best friend, Demecia Lewis. I'm excited to be a part of such a powerful book as I look at the present time when people everywhere are searching for freedom from all sorts of bondages operating in their lives. Most of us have never experienced the physical restraints such as handcuffs, leg cuffs, ropes, chains or a prison cell. Yet, spiritually we all have experienced some type of invisible chains or shackles in our lives; whether it was a childhood experience, an environment, divorce, failure in an area, and hurt in a given moment, and so on. In one form or another, we all have gone through some kind of bondage. As you read through these pages of *"Invisible Chains"*, I pray that these words will encourage, inspire, and invoke you to examine your invisible chains you may have and, ask God to break these bondages in your life for good. In Jesus name, Amen.

Shawn Lewis, M.S.
GUNNERY SERGEANT, U.S.M.C. (Retired)
S&J Lewis Consulting Solutions (Owner)
Stafford, VA

I believe this book will be an amazing read. It's stimulating and flames up your faith like no other. I am so excited for sister Demecia Lewis and pray that God would use this book to bless so many people in the kingdom of God.

Prophetess Michell Lopez
Cofounder
LUIS LOPEZ MINISTRIES INTERNATIONAL
Charlotte, NC

It gives me great joy and fulfillment to endorse this first book for my daughter. I am pleased to write this endorsement because Demecia is my daughter, but she is also a Mighty Gift to the body of Christ. This book will help those who read it and follow the instructions that are provided to grow and be more productive as you walk out your destiny. As you learn more about the strategies and tricks of the enemy of our souls (satan); You will be able to live a peaceful life of freedom. My prayer is that many will be saved, healed and delivered as a result of reading this book. May God's blessing be upon this book. You have made me proud Demecia, much love, Dad.

Apostle Dr. Robert L. Dunson
LOVE IN ACTION MINISTRIES INTERNATIONAL
Atlanta, GA

This a book that can be used as a tool to get the lost saved, but also to help them to maintain their

Endorsements

salvation. I believe maintenance is key. May the Holy Spirit use this book as an avenue to bring God's precious people out of darkness into His marvelous light. Showers of His blessings be upon you.
Dr. James R. Edmonds Jr (Ph.D.)
Founder/Apostle
KINGDOM INTERNATIONAL MINISTRIES
Alexandria, VA

After reading these beautiful words of inspiration, I would have to say that whoever reads this material will have to be encouraged and become the child of God that they desire to become. We know the author through her anointing and message in these pages has provided hope to whomever read this book and I pray you will feel the same.
Sr. Pastors Roscoe & Virginia Lane
Founders
LIVING WORD CHURCH OF GOD IN CHRIST
Rochester, NY

I must say that I am very blessed to see your kingdom work. I have known sister Demecia Lewis for many years and she has always displayed kindness and Christ-like character. I have watched her endure some trials, but exemplify faith in our Lord and Savior, Jesus Christ. This woman of God is a lover of God and Man as well as a supportive mother and wife. I am honored to be a part of her life and I am certain that what she does is inspired by the Holy Spirit. It is with great pleasure that I endorse this book.

Prophetess Isha Odom
Founder
ISHA ODOM MINISTRIES
Albany, GA

It gives us great pleasure and joy to endorse Demecia's book to the Nations and to God's people. Demecia has fought many battles and won the victory in her own life. We recommend her book, *Invisible Chains* to those who are bound by tradition, religious spirits, old ways of thinking, old mindsets, and strongholds that the enemy has used to captivate God's people. Demecia is a woman after God's own heart. *Invisible Chains* exemplifies love for God's people along with a desire for God's people to love one another and to be set free from satan's stronghold and devices. In her book, she has given us insight, revelation, wisdom, knowledge, prayer and fasting, and how to overcome obstacles. Please take the time to read this book and we guarantee you will be blessed.

Richard & Clara Brown
RICHARD BROWN MINISTRIES
Jacksonville, NC

DEDICATION

I DEDICATE THIS BOOK TO MY BEST FRIEND, deliverer, and healer, my Lord and Savior Jesus Christ, because without Him this book wouldn't be possible. I love you Heavenly Father with all my heart, mind, body and soul.

PROLOGUE

I'm a true believer that the best way to understand something is to take it from the top which I will do in this book as I ask God, who is, "The Father of Abraham, Isaac and Jacob" to give us the wisdom to break the *'Invisible Chains'*. I believe there is an anointing from God that destroys the very yoke of bondage from the enemy. This is my question for you, is there anything too hard for God? Absolutely not! So here we go saints let's get free.

'Chains' are a series, group of things, or people who were connected to each other in some way. Something that *"confines", "restrains", or "concocts"*. As I began to meditate and think about life, I think about all of the strongholds that keep us in captivity like these invisible chains used against us by demons. A few of these *chains* include addictions to drugs, alcohol, food, and sex; just to name the visible ones, but some of the less obvious are soul ties and generational curses which are invisible. Generational curses are links that have been passed down through multiple generations until the curse is recognized and broken through radical change

and having a close relationship with the Holy Spirit. Many problems families face today stem from secrets that dissipate relationships and tear families apart. Two of these problems are on the topics regarding homosexuality and molestation, because the pain is often hidden from view by the person suffering from it. This type of life practice can attach itself to the lives of the next generation. All tricks of the enemy.

Have you ever heard the saying that satan has no new tricks? It is true because he is a master deceiver, an imitator, he doesn't create, nor does he promote love. His wish is to kill you. Before he kills you, he will manipulate your life with as many lies as he can to get you to believe. So, let's be very clear, we do have an enemy; his name is satan. And he desires to keep you in chains. I'm not going to say much more about him because he gets no glory from me; just making you aware. However, you do need to recognize and understand the attacks that you endure come from him and some of the things you have lost are because of him. The word teaches us that my people perish because of the lack of knowledge (Hosea 4:6). God said, "When a thief be found he should be made to pay back seven times what he stole" (Proverbs 6:30, 31). Recognize who the 'thief' is and I don't want you to just think about materialistic things right now. I want you to think about all the days you suffered in agony with fear and worry because the enemy had stolen your joy, knowing the joy of the Lord is your strength

(Nehemiah 8:10). Now that you know it gets easier from here. You wrestle not against flesh and blood (Ephesians 6). This is a spiritual battle and the way you win is through fervent prayer, fasting, staying in faith and supplication. The Word tell us that the fervent effectual prayers of a righteous man avails much (James 5:16).

Hang on people of GOD...I pray that this book will cause you to think, help in your walk with Him, and bless your life in the name of the Lord Jesus.

I

One

The Wars in Life

I HAVE GONE THROUGH MANY FIRES IN MY life.

My life has been a trial for an extensive amount of time. All things seemed in a place of extreme standstill many times throughout my years. Have you ever felt like that? However, I believe that the same power that raised Jesus from the dead is the same power available to us today.

My main goal for this book is to glorify the Lord and to give you the tools to help you overcome. I want you to see the power of God and His signs and wonders described so clearly in Scripture, and that it would cause you to stop midstream of whatever you are doing causing you to shout, "*Hallelujah! Thank you, Jesus!*" I urge you to tell others about the power-surge anointing the Lord gives to His people, including what you will feel as you read this book the Holy Spirit gave me to write just for you.

The Holy Spirit is amazing. I believe His presence is so profound, so real, and so tangible that people will be set free from years of bondage and pain by sacrificing all to the Lord; in total surrender.

I pray that the spirit of favor falls heavily on you now. I also pray that the anointing of the Holy Spirit begins to manifest supernaturally and make you free. I write this because when I look back on my life and the things the Lord has shown me it makes me rejoice all over again.

I recalled a time in my life when I had totally surrendered my desires, fears, and setbacks all to the Lord. Well, perhaps it really wasn't a setback; I just had to learn to let go.

My parents were married at an early age in life and unfortunately, their marriage didn't last. My mother raised my siblings and I as a single parent because my dad for some reason chose to be absent. My love for him never changed and in my heart, I always had a secret wish that my dad would return home and my parents would reunite so my mom wouldn't have to work so hard. I tell you my mom is a strong woman of God and she showed her love to us in everything she did. I recall waking up one Christmas morning and my mom pulling me aside to tell me a secret. It's funny remembering how she has always found a way to make each of us feel special. The secret was at noon dad would arrive for a visit. I was ecstatic and I couldn't believe what I was hearing. This was the first time I cried tears of joy.

I didn't even know what tears of joy were but I knew I was very happy and that happiness brought

The Wars in Life

those tears. As promised my dad came home and we had a good time laughing and talking to dad about all the things which happened over the years. He apologized to us for not being there like a father should and then he asked each of us for our forgiveness, so of course we forgave him. Although at our age, we didn't understand how the trials of life could cause people to make decisions not in the best interest of anybody, but if you don't stay in Christ this is what can happen. The enemy can take you away from your family with hopes of destroying you and them. My dad was there for about a week and to my dismay they weren't going to reconcile as I had hoped. The tears I cried that day in pain when he drove away were the same tears I cried when he came home, but they felt so much different.

However, I didn't give up hope. Even when my dad would call a few times after the visit I would tell him that mom said she loved him and he would always say I love your mom too. I didn't understand how two people could love one another and not want to be together. It wouldn't be long before God showed me. Some years later, my mom met my stepdad, may he rest in peace. The joy I saw on my mom's face when she was with him I never saw before, even when my dad was home for that brief amount of time. My stepdad was a real man. My mom retired from nursing and he took care of us until we walked out the door with our own husbands. I wanted to have jealousy and resentment in my heart for him from the beginning because he wasn't my biological father. My feelings weren't possible because God had given my stepdad the personality, favor, and everything he needed to be understanding. He respected and knew that we loved my dad. This respect from him showed us his sincerity. I praised almighty God even though I was a teenager. I still had the opportunity to have a man that wasn't my biological father in my life. I'll never forget the words he told my husband when he asked him for my hand in marriage. He said, "young man if for any reason things don't work out she has a home right here. This is where you're taking her from and if you have to bring her back do it without a scratch on her." My husband said, "yes sir," and we were off to Japan to start our family. John Atkinson was the best stepfather on earth that I could ever had in my life and I celebrate now when I think about his new life over in glory with King Jesus. Surely, I will see him again. I can say for sure that I'm free from the bondage of pain and uncertainty I had as a young girl. God showed me he has a plan for our lives to prosper us and not harm us. I'm thankful now for the beautiful relationship I have with my biological dad, Apostle Robert Dunson. He prays with me and teaches me more about God's word. Look at how awesome God is and we should trust Him with absolutely everything.

The Wars in Life

What a mighty loving God we serve Saints.

Think about this for a moment: Surely if the bones of Prophet Elisha were anointed enough to bring back a dead man, I believe Almighty God through His Son, Jesus, will do the same for you as well.

Question:

Do you know how powerful it is when we work together?
Well, I say let us follow the examples in the Word of God when mighty things happen as when the Body of Christ works in unison. This is my main reason for naming this book, *"Invisible Chains"*. I believe with all of my heart we can break free, and by the end of this book, I believe this will come to pass for you, as you become refreshed and revived. As I sit here, I can't help to think how many times in our own lives, in various forms, the wars which have broken out within us that weren't right before God and man. And yes, there are many wars in life. Whether physical, spiritual or emotional. Moreover, these wars can either break us or make us.

How many times we have warred within ourselves with thoughts and temptations?
This reminds me about the life of an apostle that understood from a human perspective how it feels

and what it means to struggle with certain types of wars that can take a toll on our lives.

Apostle Paul wrote:

> **Romans 7:23 (KJV)**
> **But I see another law in my members, warring against the law of my mind, and bringing me into captivity to the law of sin which is in my members.**

This man was the great apostle Paul who wrote most of the New Testament besides Jesus who also was tempted such as common to us human beings. There is an element that I love about the Lord that helps you and I overcome these battles in our minds and hearts. As you keep reading Romans Chapter 7 you will see the incredible feats Paul accomplished as well as the struggles he had to endure. And you know what? He made it! And he made it big! If he can do it, you and I can do it. If he made it to the end of the race and fought the good fight of faith... you and I can do it as well.

LOVING ONE ANOTHER

According to Jesus we know that truth prevails. As we know, we battle with this idea frequently in life. How so?

Let me start by saying we do not **always** experience truth and justice prevailing in our lives, but

The Wars in Life

it does not mean it doesn't happen. The reality is that we live in a world that is owned by a God who has given us objective morals. This is why we know injustice when we see it. *Praise God for that*. In the same instance, there are people who do not care nor desire to know intimately the Creator who made them which would allow them to see chaos and war in their lives and to come to a place of peace and tranquility.

Regardless of that view, whether they want to know their Maker or not, the truth remains Jesus one day will come back with justice written all over His DNA to vindicate us from all the wrongs done to us. Even so, there is a responsibility we were all given when Christ ascended back up to heaven. And that responsibility was called, *Love*. I believe as a human race if we all genuinely loved one another, this world would be totally transformed. However, we know this is far from the truth at the moment as we wait for the day soon coming when the Messiah will return to earth triumphantly to march us into that time of Peace and Glory. Wow! It will be glorious.

Meanwhile, while we are here, let us as the Church of Christ show The Lord's character in modeling after Him, loving one another and not hating each other. Treating each other with kindness and respect.

John 13:34 (KJV)
A new commandment I give to you, that <u>you should love</u> one another. As I have loved you, so you also should love one another.

Galatians 6:10 (KJV)
As we have therefore opportunity, let us do good unto all men <u>especially</u> unto <u>them who are of the household of faith</u>.
(Emphasis added)

PEACE THIS IS WAR, WAR THIS IS PEACE

Living in peace is so much better than being at war.

But what happens when war knocks at the door of your heart?

What happens when peace also knocks at your heart?

Guess what? It's up to us in how we respond.

I write this because if you find yourself in a place of anger and do not want to hear what anyone nor the Holy Spirit has to say; this is not a good place emotionally or spiritually for you. And yet, in God's mercy a warming thought is He understands you. However, we must still be able to walk in the Holy Spirit with the peace Jesus bought for us with no place of interference.

The Wars in Life

On the other hand, what happens when peace comes to us while we are in a war within? Of course, it's a bit ironic because it would not take much for you or me to easily erupt even though God is operating within us. So, this tells me there is a liberty which helps us overcome since this is not God's best for anyone's life. Yet, we do not want peace to come but we desire to stay in the emotion of war. Why? Did we have enough of residing in a place so tired of life and its issues coming after us wave after wave? Do we desire to stay mad and do not want peace nor hear what God has to say?

We all have experienced weary days and it's troubling when individuals end up in this state of mind. We must realize if we do not put things in order the adversary will take a person through other avenues that will be very destructive.

There have been times I did not want freedom from the chains…and when the chains got too much for me to bear, I desired freedom to come and break every chain. Human life is a strange thing, yet beautiful.

The great thing is Jesus came to bring a life that will keep us in His peace. Don't get me wrong, anger is a healthy emotion as long as it remains in its' lane. Holy anger or righteous indignation is very useful when expressed appropriately. In this, peace can still have its reign in our hearts since this is what leads us to victory within ourselves. So, I urge you to press toward the mark and allow the Holy Spirit to help you break the bondage of any type, whether it's a false peace or a war, or whether it's out or in your circle which may disrupt your walk with Christ. I know you can make it through. Never allow the chains of cruel anger to hold you back from your "promise land" as it once did when Prophet Moses' anger caused him to disobey God and miss entering the promise land (Read Scripture Below).

Numbers 20:8-12 (NLT)
And the LORD said to Moses, "You and Aaron must take the staff and assemble the entire community. As the people watch, speak to the rock over there, and it will pour out its water. You will provide enough water from the rock to satisfy the whole community and their livestock." So Moses did as he was told. He took the staff from the place where it was kept before the LORD. Then he and Aaron summoned the people to come and gather at the rock. "Listen, you rebels!" he shouted. "Must we bring you water from this rock?" Then Moses raised his hand and struck the rock twice with the staff, and water gushed out. So the entire community and their livestock drank their fill. But the LORD said to Moses and Aaron, "Because you did not trust me enough to demonstrate my holiness to the people of Israel, you will not lead them into the land I am giving them!

The Wars in Life

Know Saints that no matter what you struggle with, remind yourself in the eyes of Christ you are a champion. I agree, we all have shortcomings that may pull us back but I pray His Holy Spirit guides us to keep moving forward. We cannot afford to give up because things get hard. The Holy Ghost is our comfort allowing us to feel there is no condemnation in Him. And without Him comforting us we would drown in our guilt. Therefore, this knowledge allows us to stimulate our senses sharp enough to pick up anything hard to discern that would set us back, recognize it and rebuke if necessary.

Romans 8:1, 2 (NKJV)
There is therefore now no condemnation to those who are in Christ Jesus, who do not walk according to the flesh, but according to the Spirit. For the law of the Spirit of life in Christ Jesus has made me free from the law of sin and death.

God the Holy Ghost guides, comforts and heals up wounds. The devil pushes, condemns, and opens up wounds.

Two

Time Ran from Me

WITH CERTAINTY, EVERYONE WOULD AGREE time is going by so fast.

Where has time gone saints? As I share this with you, no matter how you feel at this moment, know the Lord will always make up for lost time. First, never allow lost time to take away your praise and worship. Secondly, do not let lost time take away your walk with Christ. *Stand strong and focus on King Jesus* (See Ephesians 6:10). He is the one that can make up for lost time.

With conviction, I can say for sure, there were many times in my life I have allowed a foolish situation and/or silly people take away so much of my mind and time. Now don't get me wrong, I don't feel this way toward all people. However, I have to make sure that I'm always in God's presence and those who are around me are as well. Time is precious and I thank God for giving me these years.

NOT FORGOTTEN

Maybe you feel it's too late for you. Maybe you feel you are too old to do anything for the Lord and His people. Or, maybe you feel like you cannot be used by Father God because you are disabled in some kind of way. *That's a lie from the devil*. It's not too late for you *Beloved*. Always know there is nothing impossible for the Lord of all the universe. There are ways of giving to His kingdom to pursue His purpose and will. One way is giving financially to build the kingdom of God through various ministries since ministry costs money. Other types of giving are of your time and prayers. If you are able to go above and beyond that, then that is also a blessing. There is nothing like the heart of a volunteer as many say. And it's a true statement because their motive is not money-driven but love-driven. As they are filled with compassion for people; whether saved or unsaved. There is always time for us to do things for one another on this planet full of hatred, war, and addiction.

This is a great time for us as a body to come together and help one another when we are going through tough times and seasons. This is the reason I believe King Solomon was right when he penned the book of Ecclesiastes. In fact, he states in the Word of God there is a time and season for everything that happens in our lives.

Time Ran from Me

Ecclesiastes 3:1-8 (KJV)
To everything there is a season, and a time to every purpose under the heaven: A time to be born, and a time to die; a time to plant, and a time to pluck up that which is planted; A time to kill, and a time to heal; a time to break down, and a time to build up; A time to weep, and a time to laugh; a time to mourn, and a time to dance; A time to cast away stones, and a time to gather stones together; a time to embrace, and a time to refrain from embracing; A time to get, and a time to lose; a time to keep, and a time to cast away; A time to rend, and a time to sew; a time to keep silence, and a time to speak; A time to love, and a time to hate; a time of war, and a time of peace.

God is so wise and full of power. And it saddens me that so many lives have experienced so much lost time. Not to mention the many inventions not yet invented. There are so many churches and outreach centers not established. There are so many potential politicians, ministers, builders, singers, and entrepreneurs in our graves. And so much more. People have decided not to walk with Christ and made wrong choices leading to their lives cut short because of addictions. Many of them died without fulfilling their dreams that the Lord had for their lives to impact this world for His glory.

I ask you women/men of God to keep our generation as well as the generation behind us who have paved the way in their prayers and the generation ahead of us who are becoming more godless day-by-day. Too many are dying for foolish reasons. It's true, in the eyes of the LORD we are not forgotten although at times you may feel this way. And I am sure some or many of the unfortunate who died before their time thought it was too late for them and that God had forgotten them. In my heart, I think it's a lie from satan to make an individual think they are too old, too far gone, and too deep in their sin that they cannot come out and be used by the Lord God Almighty. We break those lies off of you in Christ Jesus. You are not forgotten as long as you are alive on Earth, you can still be free and used by the Almighty God.

FIGHT! AND HOLD ON!

Our responsibility is never-ending for humanity. The Bible always speaks about work we can do for the Lord. Even if someone doesn't quite believe it, nor take Him at His word, it's still true. This is why we have to hold on to the truth in these last and evil days. *Time is running out.* Tens of millions annually are dying and going to hell. My heart cries out in prayer to God for those who are tragically leaving this earth for foolish reasons that could have been prevented. My heart also goes out to the mothers who are losing their children to drugs and/

or their spending the rest of their lives in prison. It's the enemy's job to make sure to take out the men. Every man-child is a main target for the adversary to take out. To kill them or lock them up is the goal of satan and his foul kingdom. Women as well, but he is blood thirsty to remove all men since they are the head of their household when they become of age. The goal of the enemy, which he runs after fervently with enthusiasm, is taking down the head. Making sure no purpose or destiny gets fulfilled in their lives.

Saints...*Fight. Fight in prayer. Fight from your war room. Fight in the Spirit. Fight with fervor. Fight with everything you got.* We can do this together. We do not war against people, although people can make our lives impossible sometimes. Just know it is unclean foul spirits which influence people and they place wicked thoughts in their minds. Demons do not care if they are your family or friends or unknown person. They just want their contaminated will to be done and not our God's. Nevertheless, *God's will, will prevail.* Don't fight flesh with flesh; you'll lose that battle. *You fight flesh with the Holy Spirit.*

2 Corinthians 10:4, 5 (KJV)
For the weapons of our warfare are not carnal, but mighty through God to the pulling down of strong holds; Casting down imaginations, and every high thing that exalteth itself against the knowledge

of God, and bringing into captivity every thought to the obedience of Christ.

WAR CAMP

The Holy Scriptures states in Matthew's gospel there is a war which is very violent against the kingdom of heaven.

Matthew 11:12 (NKJV)
And from the days of John the Baptist until now the kingdom of heaven suffers violence, and the violent take it by force.

Our understanding according to the Holy Scriptures explains the kingdom of God is within us. Since it is within us this means we are able to reach the Holy Spirit and reign against any foul spirit causing division. In Chapter One I talked about the wars which occur in our lives, mentally, physically or spiritually that try to hold us back from God's best. However, when you're getting older and nothing is happening in your life, this is the moment that you say, *enough is enough*. Why? Because the devil does not want you to walk into your destiny. He desires for time to run out by keeping you busy with everything else while the years are flowing by, distracting you from entering into God's plans for your life.

In boot camp, the Drill Sergeant will stretch your body to the limit for what is to come. The military is preparing to build you up, not to destroy you but to mold you, causing you to become stronger than ever before, preparing you inwardly and outwardly for battle. The job requires the person to first become broken down until there is nothing left which in turn the Sergeant builds the person back up little by little. Sounds to me a bit similar in how Adonai does it. He puts us both in and through the fire until we are broken and all impurities diminish.

This kind of training requires nerves of steel.
This is not for the faint of heart.
This is not for the foolish.
This is not for the weary.
This is not for those who run when things get bad in life.
This is for those who have a deep willingness to know Him and the power of His resurrection.
This is for those who need to see the face of GOD.
This is for those who need to know how many times His heart beats.

BE STRONG IN THE LORD

The New Testament commands us to be strong in the Lord and to continue in the power of His might. Indeed, beloved, there are times we do not feel that kind of strength at the moment life is beating us up. I recall back in 2003 receiving the worst news any mother would dread to hear during a routine ultrasound. As I lay on the table anxiously awaiting to see the rapid heartbeat of our unborn daughter during the exam, the doctor seemed concerned as she continued to search for her heartbeat and to my dismay, she located her heart but there was no beat. My baby girl had passed away before I could ever see her beautiful little face. I was totally devastated and not expecting to receive this unexpected loss. I went through a deep depression and realized through prayers, and support of my loved ones God brought me out. Although I grieved for a long time, I began to eventually accept that God does not make mistakes because He is the Creator. I never questioned him although my pain was intense. I know that God has a plan for my life and I had to stand firm on that belief although I struggled at the time. It was not until a few years later that I understood His plan even more when I received my diagnoses of multiple sclerosis and fibromyalgia. I was fortunate that my sons were a little older and more independent because I had countless days stuck in bed with pain or even worse in a hospital bed. I do know that if I had a two-year-old daughter at that time it would have been very difficult for me. Nevertheless, we do all we can within us to stay strong in our faith. I declare and decree that you are free now from whatever you are going through as you read this testimony. *In Jesus' name, I command you will be free from any type of bondage including any form of strongholds now. Beloved, walk in the freedom that The Father has promised you as His children.*

Time Ran from Me

Ephesians 6:10 (NKJV)
Finally, my brethren, be strong in the Lord and in the power of His might.

Excellent is His name. The greatest power on this earth comes from all directions since the LORD our GOD is everywhere. There is nothing for you and I to fear or to worry about. *He is with us.* Again, *He is with us.* As you read this I'm believing the Holy Spirit will be moving and stirring within you to worship. Our Majesty has healed us already… Believer, you're healed. You do not have to wait for it. It is already in you…His name is *HOLY SPIRIT*. The Holy Spirit has already brought healing to you. Even as you are reading this book He desires for you to believe and not doubt. Do not allow the devil or yourself to prevent you from receiving from the Lord your God. He will stay with you all the days of your life. You will be able to tap into the Lord's presence. *Do not give up no matter what.*

Three

A New Wine Mentality

God desires for you and I to know Him intimately.

Having this knowledge will help us to understand how He thinks about us, and He cares about what we deal with daily. He cares about everything we go through in this world. He knows and feels what we are going through. Indeed, Elohim is in heaven, but He is also living within us, what a wonderful mystery. Therefore, He knows what we are going through via the avenue of our own personal and intimate emotions within. God the Holy Spirit has come to bring us a wine that is incorruptible. And this wine resides in Him and it reveals the mind of Christ for our minds. So, we may think and act like Christ. This new wine brought to us will <u>never</u> be distasteful in the mouths of people.

He is the Miracle Man and the mentality Jesus wants us to have is His Christ-like mind. This is why it is very important to make sure we show God we habitually serve Him through our lives.

Philippians 2:5 (NKJV)
Let this mind be in you which was also in Christ Jesus.

Unfortunately, countless do not believe that another side of this new wine mentality is to believe that the miracles Christ demonstrated to the people of His time and ours is for all generations. I've experienced and have seen wondrous healings and miracles on others. In my heart, I'm convinced that there is a God and His Son is alive today. The Holy Spirit will always help us see truth no matter what others may tell us. We know what truth is and the way to this truth is by reading the Bible. This was the issue that Pontius Pilate had in his time with Jesus. He asked the Lord, "What is truth?" And the Truth was standing right in front of Him.

John 14:6 (KJV)
Jesus saith unto him, I am the way, the truth, and the life: no man cometh unto the Father, but by me.

John 18:38 (KJV)
Pilate saith unto him, what is truth? And when he had said this, he went out again unto the Jews, and saith unto them, I find in him no fault at all.

A New Wine Mentality

BROKEN HOPE

All of us want more in life. It is tragic when we see a human life fall into despair and hopelessness. Whether it be a family member, a friend, a celebrity or even an enemy. Jesus cares about our eternity no matter who they are. He does not take joy in the death of the wicked since He knows they enter a place which is an eternal separation from God's grace and mercy. The book of Proverbs says it best:

Proverbs 13:12 (KJV)
Hope deferred maketh the heart sick: but when the desire cometh, it is a tree of life.

This is so true because if we have no hope the heart is full of despair. *At times, we come to a place we no longer want to wait or have our hopes remaining elsewhere, we want it now.* It's not good to feel like nothing would ever change, like a promise from God that seems light years away or desiring a way out of a tough situation. One thing I do know, we have a Jesus who can and will bring comfort to our souls. This is an awesome promise in His word which can comfort anyone if we allow it. If you ever feel broken-hearted, or sadden by a situation, or even a family member who hurt you, or died too early...think on these amazing scriptures of promise, and allow the Spirit of Christ to comfort you.

Psalms 34:18 (KJV)
The Lord is nigh unto them that are of a broken heart; and saveth such as be of a contrite spirit.

Psalms 147:3 (KJV)
He healeth the broken in heart, and bindeth up their wounds.

With all assurance, I believe God can heal anything just as He healed my husband and I. If He did it for us, He can definitely do it for you. Keep reminding yourself by His stripes you're healed. Keep trusting Him in faith and you will see it manifest. If you are feeling any of these emotions in your heart as you are reading this book know that Jesus paid the price for you over 2,000 years ago, NO matter what you are facing at this moment, remember you are healed from:

- Hopelessness
- Brokenness
- Anger
- Pride
- Betrayal
- Wrath
- Loss of things
- Drug abuse
- Deadly emotions
- Bitterness
- Unforgiveness
- Rage

A New Wine Mentality

- Alcoholism
- Sex addiction and abuse
- A broken promise
- Death of a loved one
- Despair
- Rape
- Loneliness
- False religion
- Sorcery (Witchcraft)
- Bondage(s)
- Spiritual and Mental Strongholds
- Evil spiritual chains

None of these have any power over you, unless you give it power. The devil's job is to make sure we don't see that truth. However, the King of the Universe already healed us from all of these in the list. He heals and restores today and continues to do so everyday. Having this knowledge is hopeful because it helps us remember and know that the Lord loves us and we are not facing any of these afflictions alone. And I am sure there are so many more in this list, but I mentioned just enough to show you that at the cross our broken hopes in any situation were all healed. Almighty God has come to bring *freedom from these chains*.

John 8:36 (KJV)
If the Son therefore shall make you free, ye shall be free indeed.

2 Corinthians 3:17 (NLT)
For the Lord is the Spirit, and wherever the Spirit of the Lord is, there is FREEDOM.

LET FREEDOM RING

This *Freedom* is true. This *Freedom* brings lives back together again. There is nothing too far gone that cannot be brought back to union. We, as a Body of Believers have seen and heard with our own eyes how our Father brings people and families together; even nations.

He has the power to do this in marriages as well. And yes, there are times many marriages, lives, relationships have fallen apart and have remained this way. Does this mean that God didn't have the power to do it or paid favoritism toward the ones that did make it? *God forbids. He never fails.* Things still happen. Keep in mind we are fallen man living in a fallen world. Nonetheless, Holy Spirit is still at work to this day He is not a force but a person. When Messiah comes for His Bride, the Church, He will bring justice to all.

I apologize in advance, if I don't have the words of comfort or the reason these things still do happen. However, let's not focus on the ones that did not make it but celebrate the ones that did by His power and Spirit.

Say this prayer:

A New Wine Mentality

PRAYER

Jesus, I come before your presence and I want to thank you for all the good things you have done for me (and my family). I repent for any doubts, or, if I blamed you in any way for the situations that have happened in my life. My life is yours and I know that my hopes, dreams, and freedoms are in you my Lord. You will never let me down or stop me from getting the best in this life. Holy Spirit, help me to keep on trusting you and allowing you to comfort me. Help me Spirit of God to break off anything in my life that is not from you or of your spirit. Wash me and cleanse me in the name of Jesus! Thank you, Father, for being my God and friend. I love you. In Jesus name, I pray, Amen.

Now that you have prayed that prayer. Get ready Friend, you are about to enter the realm of true Freedom from all sorts of chains in your life. The devil has no rights in your life. These rights belong to your Maker. In the physical realm, you keep standing strong believing in the Word of God. And nothing would be impossible for you. This is the will of God. Although, many will not believe it. Here is a Scripture reference that attests what I am saying,

Psalms 37:4 (KJV)
Delight thyself also in the Lord; and he shall give thee the desires of thine heart.

Psalms 149:4 (KJV)
For the Lord taketh pleasure in his people: he will beautify the meek with salvation

Jeremiah 29:11 (KJV)
For I know the thoughts that I think toward you, saith the Lord, thoughts of peace, and not of evil, to give you an expected end.

From my view, this is another way of seeing the n*ew wine mentality*. I am sure there are many other revelations to see what Jesus was meaning about putting new wine in new wine skins so they would not burst. Which is so true. When you look at it from a spiritual perspective you can see that we cannot mix the old with the new (i.e., The Old Testament and the New Testament). You cannot mix law and grace. In fact, Galatians 3 says if we are under the law we are under a curse.

Galatians 3:10 (KJV)
For as many as are of the works of the law are under the curse: for it is written, cursed is every one that continueth not in all things which are written in the book of the law to do them.

A New Wine Mentality

As the Holy Bible relates to us the importance to keep up Christ-likeness in the "bottle" of His presence, with assurance I can see it's for our best interest. I have never known God to try and hurt us in any way, shape, or form. In fact, His interest is to break us and then mold us back into His way and shape. Our will cannot prevail when being a born again Christian. Our lives are not our own we are all bought with a price (Read 1 Corinthians 6:20). In addition, Jesus taught if we walk in His ways our "spiritual wine" will be preserved.

Matthew 9:17 (KJV)
Neither do men put new wine into old bottles: else the bottles break, and the wine runneth out, and the bottles perish: but they put new wine into new bottles, and both are preserved.

No believer according to this passage should ever allow their 'bottle' to break and their 'wine' to run out if you will. We must stay very protective in what the Lord gives us. In my life (and I pray you model after me in this) I hold prayer at a high regard when things are well and not so well. In prayer, I can say it brings people and relationships back together.

Hopefully, I can help you to understand when the Spirit of Christ hears that you need deliverance from something which can kill you or destroy you in a tremendous way. Just call on the name of the

Lord Jesus. He will rescue you. He is there regardless of how you feel. The book of Galatians said it best when Apostle Paul penned:

I John 4:7 (NKJV)
Beloved, let us love one another, for love is of God; and everyone who loves is born of God and knows God.

IV

Four

A Fight for Your Mind

*E*VOLUTION STATES THAT WE ALL CAME TO being by some other means than creation. Further, other philosophies have come to bring another way of how we came into existence. False religions and cultures tried to brainwash us into believing there isn't a God and that it's all in our head. If this is the case, then we are a people most miserable. Interestingly, I have heard great men say some off the wall things that makes no sense at all. We sure need wisdom in these last days.

Let me remind you we serve a God that sits high and looks low, there is nothing we can do to separate us from his love. In death, He's there. In life, He's there; in good times and bad times He's still there. He's available every day. So, if you call from the depths of your heart for freedom from strongholds in your life, then look to the One who is able to deliver you, heal you, and make you free.

HE WILL NEVER LEAVE YOU

Listen to what He says about you.

"I AM the Potter; you are the clay. I designed you before the foundation of the world. I arrange the events of each day to form you into this preconceived pattern. My everlasting love is at work in every event. Not some things but everything includes Me. Even the things you don't pray to Me about, from My love I still do it for you. Either you think I AM not aware, or you think it's too hard for Me. Let Me assure you my child, nothing is too hard for me at all. Nothing in your life whether good or bad is hidden from Me. I've instructed you through My Word (Jesus) to cast your cares upon Me because I care for you. I've given you dominion and authority over all things in my Son Jesus' name."

Romans 8:37-39 (NKJV)
Yet in all these things we are more than conquerors through Him who loved us. For I am persuaded that neither death nor life, nor angels nor principalities nor powers, nor things present nor things to come, nor height nor depth, nor any other created thing, shall be able to separate us from the love of God which is in Christ Jesus our Lord.

A Fight for Your Mind

Jeremiah 32:27 (NKJV)
Behold, I am the Lord, the God of all flesh. Is there anything too hard for Me?

I Peter 5:7 (NKJV)
Casting all your care upon Him, for He cares for you.

MENTAL AWARENESS

Do you remember that commercial years ago, about a person throwing an egg into a hot frying pan followed by, "A mind is a terrible thing to waste," as the egg cooks violently? Well, it's the same in the kingdom of Christ. Our minds have been from the beginning of time the field for war and battle. This is a major reason we must <u>surrender</u> our minds to the framework of God's way of thinking. His wisdom is so necessary in today's world but no one is listening. The Church must realize everything starts in our mind. The devil does not manifest anytime he wants and makes us do anything. There are occurrences that we have seen or heard about demons manifesting themselves triggering a person to do certain activities you and I know aren't appropriate. What the 'son of perdition' does is place thoughts in our minds along with his fallen angels to bring trouble and confusion knowing the Word does not work like that (See 1 Corinthians 14:33).

We are the ones that have to make the decision not to do nor say the thoughts we are being influenced to manifest. All human life on earth will be held accountable for EVERY word which proceeds out of their mouths.

Romans 3:4 (NKJV)
Certainly not! Indeed, let God be true but every man a liar. As it is written: "That you may be justified in your words, and may overcome when you are judged."

Temptations are no joke. The devil is real. He is not playing with us at all. He is on a rampage to kill us all and he will keep others alive to do his bidding. Numbers of people do not think they are being used and/or influenced to do his will through their lives, but they are. Sadly, literally billions are not in a place of salvation with the Holy Spirit living within them. Over 2.3 billion out of 7.3 billion souls on earth are professing Christians in the world, and so many more are coming to Christ annually. Still, out of that number only hundreds of millions are born again. There is a war in our minds influencing our decision-making. On a greater scale, we are losing. What makes me say this? The reason is that there are innumerable Christians dealing with so many chains of bondage. These chains are invisible and difficult to perceive. On the other hand, we are in a place in Christ Jesus to help us see the truth from all angles, and satan's lies from all corners, as the enemy's lies have one perspective. The Holy One sees truth from numerous perspectives.

A Fight for Your Mind

THE GATEKEEPER

As we know, the gates of Zion are under attack. Our responsibility is to make sure nothing penetrates through or has a gateway, no matter what avenue it tries to take. You are the gatekeeper of your soul and spirit. Gates are mentioned in the Bible. Some are spiritual, while others are physical, but the gates I'm referring to are these three below:
- Eye gate
- Ear gate
- Mouth gate

In the four Gospels, Jesus lists three important gates.
- Lust of the eyes
- Lust of the flesh
- The pride of life

These are associated with our eyes, ears, heart, mind, and tongue. Eyes lust after people and things. Our ears lust for gossip. Our heart, mind, and tongue lusts to say and think boastful and prideful things. High-mindedness and high pride will kill a person quickly when it is done before the eyes of our God. In history, we read about men and women who have boasted great things out of their mouths, and it took the master of heaven to humble them. The Bible talks about us being humble from our own accord, or the Lord will humble us. Trust me when I tell you it is better for you and I to humble ourselves.

Do it because when our creator does it, it hurts. The Bible and our own history have shown everlasting consequences of those entering hell, never to come out. To you, it may seem too far-fetched or arrogant. However, when you read the sacred passages in the Holy Word of God, you will see it is evident that there is a real hell when one passes on without being saved. In example after example in the Old Testament, we read about prophets going to hell and coming back, given another chance to do the will of God. The verse in Jonah below will remind you of how serious Almighty God is when he commands us to do something. Let's see what the prophet Jonah had to say on the matter when he didn't obey the Lord about going to Nineveh with a word that could save thousands of souls from everlasting torment.

Jonah 2:1-7 (KJV)
Then Jonah prayed unto the LORD **his God out of the fish's belly, and said, I cried by reason of mine affliction unto the L**ORD**, and he heard me; out of the belly of hell cried I, and thou heardest my voice. For thou hadst cast me into the deep, in the midst of the seas; and the floods compassed me about: all thy billows and thy waves passed over me. Then I said, I am cast out of thy sight; yet I will look again toward thy holy temple. The waters compassed me about, even to the soul: the depth closed**

A Fight for Your Mind

me round about, the weeds were wrapped about my head. I went down to the bottoms of the mountains; the earth with her bars was about me forever: yet hast thou brought up my life from corruption, O LORD my God. When my soul fainted within me I remembered the LORD: and my prayer came in unto thee, into thine holy temple.

Mentioning these things may sound a bit brash but it is still the truth. We are the gatekeepers and we are the ones who will decide what comes in and out of our gates. As you have just read about Jonah, know he was the gatekeeper of the word God gave him to speak to the people. And it's incredible how he was not willing to release the word to the city. All those lives in the entire city would have gone into ruins and hurled into hell if he kept the prophetic word to himself. Simply because he was willing to keep the gate of his mouth shut. All those souls including their blood would've been on his hands. *Deadly*. In the same instance, if the Lord speaks to you and gives you a word for someone, do not keep it to yourself…but give it. Why? Because with that word given you may save a life from hell.

I urge you to stay focused on the King asking Him for any type of courage in your walk as you go about your day. Life is not easy with God so imagine it even harder without Him. *But you got this*. You will have days of struggles but without these struggles you will not learn experience. Experience is what is going to propel you into your purpose. Wisdom will increase in you when your relationship is serious with Christ. Sacrifice is a necessary trait in your members. It would take you to a greater height because you are telling the Lord by your actions you are serious about Him. You are displaying to Him in your living that He is number one in your heart, mind and soul. No one else matters to you but God. He desires that from us but we don't give Him our best every single day. Yes, we fall short but it doesn't mean we have to stay there. *Zion*. Push back the darkness and allow the *Fire* of the *Holy Ghost* to burn within and out of you in the name of *Jesus*.

Matthew 3:11 (NKJV)
I indeed baptize you with water unto repentance, but He who is coming after me is mightier than I, whose sandals I am not worthy to carry. He will baptize you with the HOLY SPIRIT and FIRE.

Five

*Was I Ever Going To Be Healed? *

THIS TITLE IS A QUESTION MANY ASK THEMselves in the privacy of their hearts.

God hears it all. This was a question I asked myself many times as well about my diagnoses of multiple sclerosis and fibromyalgia. Just from the experiences that I have shared with you, I know that God is a healer. I am so very thankful to share with you the good news that I received 2 years ago after I had taken an MRI test. My neurologist told me the lesions in my brain had decreased in ways that he has never seen before and the decision was mine to start taking the medication to treat my earlier diagnosis. Saints, I remember that day so vividly because my heart filled with joy. Does this mean that I'm healed from these things? By faith, yes. Often, some find it unbelievable and they revert back to the question asked by many mentioned above. Many feel it's doubt and unbelief to think this way, feeling less of a Christian somehow when we hear another believer speaking in this way. We all have thought this before within ourselves. As we see others from different parts of the country and the world suffering in their bodies with all types of diseases and sicknesses, it breaks my heart. Being sick with cancer or other types of fatal infections takes a huge toll on a life. Family and friends get affected like none other, and predominantly, the individual who's sick, yearning in their hearts for healing, as soon as one receives prayer. Sadly, some do not get healed at all. This does not mean that Jesus does not care.

Occasionally, we witness via television or some type of media channel the healing of a person(s) with much rejoicing in the air. *I praise God for that.* This tells me there is still hope since the Bible states in the New Testament that the Lord does not play favoritism with anyone. We should celebrate this idea, "What if?" If there is *faith,* the Spirit of the Lord can work with that. YAHWEH desires for you to believe. He says it repetitively from Genesis to Revelation to believe Him, and to believe in Him when He says something to you or me through the prophet(s). Think about it: it feels good when we say something and others believe instead of calling you a false witness. It hurts when we know something happened to us is true, but when we express it to others, they are quick to say we are dishonest. This reminds me of the blind man in the gospels who was before the Sanhedrin and they kept badgering who healed him because they didn't believe him or Jesus.

Was I Ever Going To Be Healed?

John 9:13-34 (NKJV)

They brought him who formerly was blind to the Pharisees. Now it was a Sabbath when Jesus made the clay and opened his eyes. Then the Pharisees also asked him again how he had received his sight. He said to them, "He put clay on my eyes, and I washed, and I see." Therefore, some of the Pharisees said, "This Man is not from God, because He does not keep the Sabbath." Others said, "How can a man who is a sinner do such signs?" And there was a division among them. They said to the blind man again, "What do you say about Him because He opened your eyes?" He said, "He is a prophet." But the Jews did not believe concerning him, that he had been blind and received his sight, until they called the parents of him who had received his sight. And they asked them, saying, "Is this your son, who you say was born blind? How then does he now see?" His parents answered them and said, "We know that this is our son, and that he was born blind; but by what means he now sees we do not know, or who opened his eyes we do not know. He is of age; ask him. He will speak for himself." His parents said these *things* because they feared the Jews, for the Jews had agreed already that if anyone confessed *that* He *was* Christ, he would be put out of the synagogue. Therefore, his parents said, "He is of age; ask him." So they again called the man who was blind, and said to him, "Give God the glory! We know that this Man is a sinner." He answered and said, "Whether He is a sinner *or not* I do not know. One thing I know: that though I was blind, now I see." Then they said to him again, "What did He do to you? How did He open your eyes?" He answered them, "I told you already, and you did not listen. Why do you want to hear *it* again? Do you also want to become His disciples?" Then they reviled him and said, "You are His disciple, but we are Moses' disciples. We know that God spoke to Moses; *as for* this *fellow,* we do not know where He is from." The man answered and said to them, "Why, this is a marvelous thing, that you do not know where He is from; yet He has opened my eyes! Now we know that God does not hear sinners; but if anyone is a worshiper of God and does His will, He hears him. Since the world began it has been unheard of that anyone opened the eyes of one who was born blind. If this Man were not from God, He could do nothing." They answered and said to him, "You were completely born in sins, and are you teaching us?" And they cast him out.

John 14:1 (NKJV)
Let not your heart be troubled; you believe in God, believe also in Me.

John 16:8, 9 (NKJV)
And when He has come, He will convict the world of sin, and of righteousness, and of judgment: of sin, because they do not believe in Me...

Pay attention to the extent Jesus went to be believed in John's gospel. The Holy Spirit embraces on so many levels through the apostles how much The Lord Jesus desires your belief, even to this day, emphasizing that it's a natural trait to have this kind of heart toward Him about the kingdom of faith. Faith is a very important factor. As we read the Holy Scriptures from beginning to end, the Word germinates how God desires so much to heal His children to the degree He knew He could die a torturous death by doing such miracles, as He did. In addition, we read in Hebrews 11 that without faith, we cannot please Him.

Hebrews 11:6 (NKJV)
But without faith it is impossible to please Him, for he who comes to God must believe that He is, and that He is a rewarder of those who diligently seek Him.

I am sure that the blind man never thought he would be healed and the Lord always showed Himself strong in that blind man's life. His parents must have rejoiced seeing their own son able to see for the first time. Who wouldn't feel like rejoicing and give God all the praise for your entire life doing an act like that? Additionally, when He heals your family member or a friend, it is both physically and spiritually with His Great Salvation power. *It's wonderful.*

Saving souls Beloved is the greatest miracle. When I see someone, who is as cold as an iceberg, be melted away by the Loving healing power of God, it astonishes me greatly.

What a love.
What a God.

There is no one like Him and to say that there is such an insult; it's ridiculous. The evil one has tried so many times to mimic our Father. It's pathetic. What a joke when someone deceives millions of people by mimicking God or Jesus, when the Lord already came and left. *What foolishness to the highest degree.* Jesus came to bring healing. Jesus came to bring love, grace and mercy. "There is no condemnation for those who are in Christ trying not to fulfill the works of the flesh but to run after the Spirit" (Romans 8).

What brings me to a place of awe is when someone who has seen that the Lord is good and when the Lord healed them and blessed them pay

Him thanks by leaving Him and goes back into the world; *'tsk, tsk'*. And they expect the Lord to heal and make them whole by doing this? This is what the writer of Hebrews had to say about an evil heart of unbelief when we abandon the Lord.

Hebrews 3:12 (NKJV)
Beware, brethren, lest there be in any of you an evil heart of unbelief in departing from the living God…

THRUST FORWARD

My prayer for you is that you will stay in Christ no matter what happens to you. Do not give up, realize you can make it knowing He is with you. His character in the Word of the Lord has shown us that He will never leave you or forsake you. He is always there whether you feel Him or not. Does not matter if you see Him or not, He is always there listening and watching over you. You cannot escape Him. Let's see what king David had to say about the Lord watching and listening to us.

Psalms 139:8 (NKJV)
If I ascend into heaven, You are there; If I make my bed in hell, behold, You are there.

I pray this does not scare you, but comfort you to know He is watching over you with His holy angels assigned to your life to make sure you and your family stay protected.

WHO SAID THE LORD DOES NOT CARE?

In your mind, you may feel the Lord does not care about you or what's going on around you or even in the affairs of this world but this is untrue. He is always involved with us. What bothers you, bothers Him. What hurts you, hurts Him. Sometimes we think He isn't interested in our issues but in reality, it is a lack of having a personal relationship with him. It could be a lack of faith which I am sure we can conjure up different opinions, theories and ideas. For this reason, for someone to know God, he would need to know His character enough to perceive from the perspective of love. He is not like us in many ways.

Jesus will never leave us as orphans and treat us bad. *Man does that*.
Jesus will never say hurtful words when He is angry. *Man does that*.
Jesus will never play games with our emotions. *Man does that*.
Jesus does not throw things in our faces to hurt us in return. *Man does that*.
Jesus does not hold a record of our wrongs. *Man does that*; and the list goes on.

That is *not* the Heavenly Father I know. The World portrays Him as a tyrant or some type of imaginary being. *What a bunch of nonsense.* Saints, do not believe everything you hear. Examine and search the word of God out for yourself. Get to know Him by reading His Word and in much prayer. I guarantee you will see an excellent side of the Lord you never would imagine in your wildest dreams. God is so good even when we go through the toughest and most hurtful, loneliest moments.

Does it feel like He is there in the times of trouble? *Not always.*

However, He still is and always will be there. And when you hold on long enough, you will see without a shadow of a doubt He has established you through it all. *He is our redeemer in our circumstances. He is the One who makes us whole. He is our bondage breaker. He is the stronger man who breaks strongholds with the brightness of His coming.*

Keep these words in your heart and ponder them. You are not alone. It is not His will to leave you alone nor leave you sick. He will come to you; just ask. It is His will to heal, deliver, and set people free. Again, the Lord cares or He would not waste His time on us (1 Peter 5:7). Sadly, billions globally do not give Him the glory He deserves nor do they care to do so. *He is here now, even as you are reading this book.*

Eventually, billions will see Him face to face one day. We will either see Him as GOD, the Judge given into condemnation, or as GOD, the Father given into everlasting life.

Prophet Joshua had it right when he said, "… choose this day whom you will serve?" Friend, I say to you the same thing. Choose this day whom you will serve.

Wait, I'll help you.

Choose and serve God.

If you are one of the ones who have chosen God, choose to keep dwelling in His presence. The days are about to get even more evil. Sound doctrine isn't received by most. Witness how Americans and people abroad are going to have a lower tolerance for what is sound and peaceful for what is loud and pugnacious. We have to keep praying and prophesying the words of the Almighty. Speak what He is speaking and do what He is doing. Allow His will and not ours.

We can do it.

In fact, doing His will makes it a lot easier for Him to usher us into His healing presence. How so? There is nothing hindering us!

So, as for the question asked in this chapter, was I ever going to be healed? In a resounding voice, I declare, *"YES"! By His stripes, we already are.*

PRAYER

Thank you, my Lord Jesus, for helping me choose you above everything and everyone. Give me Your wisdom and understanding according to

Was I Ever Going To Be Healed?

Proverbs 4:7 to keep wisdom as the principle thing and in everything I get, to get understanding. Holy Ghost, you are the one who will help me choose what to place before my heart…which is You. Let your Spirit Father break out all over my life and take me to a new place in you. Flow like a river within my heart. I know you are my river. You are my life source who comforts me when things seem dead all around me. Allow me to keep placing you first in all I do and think. Thank you so much for being there for me. In Jesus' name, Amen.

VI

Six

The Man Who Saved Me

JESUS IS THE ONE THAT GETS ALL THE GLORY for the life He's given me.

Although my family has been there for me through thick and thin, it is mind-boggling how Father God placed things back into order when things would fall apart. I give Him all the honor and the glory for what He has done and still doing to this day; for me and others. Since He did it for me I know in my heart He can transform any marriage or relationship of any sort back into proper alignment. This is the reason we need to seek after the prophetic so we can see things beginning to align before they do. We must also use discernment so we can protect ourselves from the wickedness of unclean spirits operating through the life of a sinner and a carnal Christian.

The Lord saved us for a reason. Not to hurt us but because He wanted us to love Him with all we got and to love our neighbor as ourselves; like family.

SPIRIT POINT: I urge you Reader to keep trusting Him when you feel like throwing in the towel. We live in a fast-paced world with 20 million decisions we have to make a day. Although I am exaggerating, we know it's not that far from our own experiences when we get hit from all sides causing us to want Him more.

One of the most important decisions to make is receiving Jesus Christ as Lord and Savior. This is an eternal decision which would affect all human life as we know it. Our prayers for you Friend is to be saved.

II Corinthians 6:2 (NKJV)
…Behold, now is the accepted time; behold, now is the day of salvation.

If you are pricked in your heart desiring Jesus as your Lord and Savior, then please refer to Appendix A in the back of this book and repeat the **prayer of salvation** with all your heart.

I believe your best days are ahead, never behind, since there is always more. You'll be happy you did. The cool thing about being saved is you and I get to familiarize ourselves with the God of Family. He is a real Father. Moreover, He will take you to places you would not even dream of, nor will it come to mind what He would do for you. Sorry to say, in the days we live in all we do is search for the hand of the Lord instead of His heart. We want to receive things but not be a giver of things. Funny how the

Lord can use us for His glory with many wanting to use God just for the benefits given to them which hurts my heart deeply.

Imagine someone being in your circle just because of what you have. Their hearts are far from you even if they break bread with you. Wolves in sheep's clothing. We must be discerning.

Proverbs 23:7 (NKJV)
For as he thinks in his heart, so is he. "Eat and drink!" he says to you, but his heart is not with you.

Matthew 6:33 (NKJV)
But seek first the kingdom of God and His righteousness, and all these things shall be added to you.

THE SPIRIT OF BETRAYAL

Betrayal: *is the breaking or violation of a presumptive contract, trust, or confidence that produces moral and psychological conflict within a relationship among people, between organizations or between people and organizations.*

Saints, betrayal is so heart breaking when you think about its definition. What a terrible thing to happen to anyone. I can imagine how the Messiah must've felt in the garden of Gethsemane when Judas came up to Him and betrayed Him for some money; with a kiss included. *That's atrocious.* However, before we focus on how wicked Judas treated His God. My question is, "How many times (if we are honest with ourselves) have we betrayed Jesus in some way or another?" We could have done this in our minds and hearts or even physically by walking away from Christ.

This is not something we want to do unto the Lord on purpose; but at least once in our lives we have done so. Whether we were in the world or in the Kingdom, I would like to say to you Beloved, may the love of God and all His sweetness overtake you. Bear in mind, it is never a good idea to betray anyone since it hurts beyond comprehension. Let's be a people full of integrity with respect for one another. Jesus likes that idea better. If you happen to bump into someone in the church or the world with the spirit of betrayal, (i.e., gossip, false lies, etc.), as a woman or man of God we have the authority to share with them the truth in love. Not to break the person down destroying their spirits but to bring clarity and restoration with compassion.

THE MAN WHO SAVED ME FROM ME

Mentioning compassion reminds me of the awesome things Jesus has done for me when I didn't deserve it. What an incredible Father we love and serve. Believe me when I tell you the Lord has saved me from me. The decisions I have made in my past would've taken me down the wrong path.

But I am here to say, with a heart of gratitude, thank you Lord for placing people in my life to help me! Keep trusting in the Lord and watch your life shift for the better. There is no one in the universe who could *ever* compare to *Him*.

Psalms 117:2 (NKJV)
For His merciful kindness is great toward us, and the truth of the Lord endures forever. Praise the Lord!

I am so excited how the promises of the Bible radiate through these verses. He has blessed me with an awesome family and friends in Christ. I am so thankful. When I ponder this, I notice many in my circle and abroad do not feel the same. In fact, there are a lot of born again believers who are not thankful for their lives. They're too busy looking at the *now* instead of what is to come. Lies do not belong to our God or us but to satan who's the father of it. As Jesus said, when he speaks lies he speaks from his own nature. We are not to believe what we *always* see in front of us. It requires one to stand back and allow oneself to see the bigger picture. At times, it feels like when we are going through (as king David did in the Psalms) we panic as if there is no end to it. We get disheartened and discouraged in our hearts. Remember…

That Christ said,

John 14:27 (NKJV)
Peace I leave with you, My peace I give to you; not as the world gives do I give to you. Let not your heart be troubled, neither let it be afraid.

However, the passages in the New Covenant states we are to believe and not doubt. It's not a good feeling when turmoil is so high you cannot see the end of a bad situation. Discern the times as the scripture says for the days are evil. And if we are not careful we may fall into those kinds of traps. Traps of fruitlessness and bleakness. Traps of entering into mental or spiritual bondage without any freedom. It's very comforting to hear Jesus will never leave us nor abandon us, for surety our trials are for a short moment.

WISDOM FOR THE ASKING

In the long run, we gain experience and wisdom. I have heard many times over that wisdom comes with age. *Ha-ha*. I know several that need to sign up for Jesus' wisdom classes. Because I don't find that to always be true. I am sure on a grander scale this is factual, but in this country and abroad, when you turn on the television, or read the newspaper and see the foolish things going on it contradicts that statement. Hence, why Apostle James of our Lord Jesus stated by the leading of the Spirit to write to us asking for His wisdom, since He knew all of humanity needs it.

Proverbs 4:7 (NKJV)
Wisdom is the principal thing; Therefore, get wisdom. And in all your getting, get understanding.

James 1:5 (NKJV)
If any of you lacks wisdom, let him ask of God, who gives to all liberally and without reproach, and it will be given to him.

There is so much I can write about the Man who has saved me. And as you know this Man is our Lord Jesus Christ. Trusting Him is very wise to do. I know a lot of people in the world that are atheists or agnostics even in other religions which see Jesus as a stumbling block. Now goes the saying, He definitely chooses the foolish things of the world to confound anyone who claims wisdom before His presence. This is so no man can boast and take the credit at all whatsoever. No one can try to take any of the glory away from our God in their strength, just so they can vaunt what they've done it's by their own power as many have done so in the past. Although many try, they always fall short with strong failure. In my mind, why would someone try to fight the God who made them? Instead of emanating respect to the God of Israel.

**1 Corinthians 1:27 (KJV)
But God hath chosen the foolish things of the world to confound the wise; and God hath chosen the weak things of the world to confound the things which are mighty…**

I praise God for opening up my eyes to so much truth. There are no words to express how I feel toward the one who has shown me love in abundance and opened the doors for my husband and I. But I know one thing. If He did it for me, He will definitely do it for you. We are one in the Spirit. Well, we are supposed to be anyway. You will stand in the liberty Jesus paid by dying on that cross for our salvation. You are already free from all types of demonic chains of oppression and regions of imprisonment.

Say this prayer:

PRAYER FROM IMPRISONMENT

I declare and decree that I am already saved and filled with the Holy Ghost. I have authority and power to come against anything not aligned with the Word of God. And I thank you Jesus for dying for me and making me free from all types of strongholds and afflictions. I bind the works of satan trying to stop me from walking into my destiny. I release the promises of God instead, in the name of Jesus. I come against all types of disease and sickness. I am free from it all. Lord you speak

The Man Who Saved Me

those things that are not as though they already are. I thank You in advance no matter what I face for You are with me. I am not imprisoned. I am not depressed. I am not going to believe the lie. I will speak the words of Christ and receive salvation of the Lord God. Thank You so much for saving me. I love you Lord. In the name of Jesus. Amen.

VII

Seven
Understanding Your Purpose

I GET EXCITED EVERY TIME I REMEMBER THE goodness of God. Do you?

I remember the day when I received the baptism of the Holy Spirit. I was 24 years old in my first year of marriage in Okinawa, Japan, where we attended a wonderful Holy Ghost filled church called *Agape Fellowship Revival Center*. I remember our first visit; *Oh my, it was on fire. We praised the Lord and it was so liberating.* I was in a place where I felt very happy and free in this service. I had a glimpse of my husband operating for the first time in the gift of tongues. When we went home that night, I felt so excited, but I must admit feeling a little jealous. In my thoughts, I said, *"Lord I love you, but I want the power in the gift of tongues as well."*

So, I began studying about it, and asking the saints about the power of God and how to receive it. I kept hearing them say, *"all you have to do is ask Him."* So, I did, but nothing happened. All week I pondered repeatedly, praying and asking, waiting to receive. One time, someone told me to just keep saying, "*HalleluYAH*" out loud over and over and then my language would change and I would receive it then. Well it wasn't working, so I became a little discouraged. Virtually, I understood my purpose and what it meant for me as a powerful Christian because in my mind I was saying I'm saved, and in the same instance asking, "Why am I not speaking in my heavenly language"?

Well a few weeks later on Saturday night, I was getting ready for bed, and in my spirit, I kept hearing, "If you go you will receive it." I'm thinking, "Go where? When"? Moreover, as I was still pondering these questions in my heart, I was already planning to go to church early in the morning.

As I am preparing to go to church, I am thinking to myself, "Hmm, Am I supposed to go somewhere else"? By this time, we get to church and I tell you the truth, the words I heard weeks before felt strong in my spirit, so strong that I can feel it now, as I continue to hear, "If you go you will receive it"!

Well, we attended church service, having a wonderful time in the Lord and now it's getting close to the end, and I am feeling a little disappointed because I went there with a spirit of expectation knowing for sure I was going to receive something from the Lord. All of a sudden, God moved on the heart of an evangelist who was there by the name of Clara. She received direction from the Lord to anoint everyone with oil. Subsequently, we all lined up in the center aisle. They made it clear that they were not going to pray this time, but walk pass each one of us as they would anoint us with oil until they reached the end of the line. And once they touched us with the oil we returned to our seats.

Now Beloved, I'm in this line and the line is moving fast. In desperation, I walked up to be anointed with the blessed oil. As soon as I was touched with the oil on my head and received the anointing, like normal, I took one step toward my seat. As I tried my best to walk toward the pew where I was sitting, suddenly, *the Holy Spirit took a hold of me, as if a person literally grabbed you but invisible. An amazing joy took over my heart and I could not contain it, I went down to the floor.*

The Spirit of God was all over me, blessing me, filling me up.

I do not have the words to describe the immeasurable amount of joy I was feeling. I was trying to say, "*HalleluYAH*", but my tongue was rolling repetitively, saying something I had never heard before. **WOW**. The Holy Spirit had taken over and I heard my prayer language for the first time. *I knew for a fact, without a shadow of a doubt, I received my baptism in and by the Holy Spirit Himself. Amen.*

Our God did what He said He would do. Afterward, I kept praising the Lord in the car, and by the time I got home, I had received my prayer language in full. *In my Christian walk, I remember in church service saying one tongue repetitively, not anymore. God is so marvelous.* How true the words of John Newton's song published in 1779, when he wrote,

"Amazing grace, how sweet the sound, who saved a wretch like me, I once was lost but now I'm found, I was blind but now I see."

He endowed me with power from on high and has done so many more wonderful things since then. Who wouldn't serve a God like our God? He's faithful and true. I pray that this testimony will encourage and inspire you to know that God has perfect timing to bless you; He does answer prayer.

THE IMPORTANCE OF PURPOSE

Having purpose in life is so meaningful and vibrant. It brings a shine to the eye and a glow to the heart. It causes one to feel there is meaning for their lives. *The feeling of one prophesying to us about something we did not share with anyone hearing it from the lips of another about the plans of God for your life is so awe-inspiring.*

Psalms 20:4 (NKJV)
May He grant you according to your heart's desire, and fulfill all your purpose.

Jeremiah 29:11 (NKJV)
For I know the thoughts that I think toward you, says the Lord, thoughts of peace and not of evil, to give you a future and a hope.

Understanding Your Purpose

We agree that the Spirit indeed speaks to our spirit to guide us. This is important because we need this so bad. With this in mind, we can understand the Lord makes a big deal to speak to us about His purpose manifested in our lives to reach our destiny. Having discernment will help catapult you into this gift when you stay in prayer. Fasting is another way of killing your flesh so you can die to self and allow God to speak to you as you will hear with more clarity. The gifts given to us help us to bless others. Our purpose in life is to become a blessing.

We were never created to purely be a reservoir, but a channel. Let me urge you to understand what God is saying to you in this season. Please do not miss your season. There is someone in this world that is waiting for your arrival. There is someone needing you now. When you meet others, I am sure you will be given a word from the Spirit of Christ for that person. *Only Believe. Believe the impossible. And watch God do it.*

GOD IS ABLE TO BRING PURPOSE AND BREAK STAGNATION

It is a scary thought knowing there is no reason or purpose of why you are alive. I would rather live than survive. Purpose helps you feel there is more to this life than the everyday circle just to wake up and do it again. This King of Existence can catapult someone out from depression and boredom into joy and freedom. These emotions are used by satan to drift you or someone you know into complacency, attaching other toxic emotions to it. *I pray that you will stand fast in the Holy Ghost.* There is nothing that He cannot do for you. You will make it in this crazy world. Trust me when I tell you, my husband and I have gone through so much. I tell you what, if we didn't build our relationship with Christ by reading, praying, and fasting with consecration, then we would've thrown in the towel a long time ago. If I can do it, you can do it.

The Lord God does not play favoritism with anyone. He loves us all the same. No one is better than anyone. There is no one like the Lord in all the earth. Put your faith in Him and keep it there. The devil cannot mess with your faith because it's invisible. The devil cannot touch it. This faith channel is by the Spirit of Elohim (my Lord). We are to learn to hate the darkness and love His marvelous light. It does not matter if things feel like a reservoir with no change…keep being *AGGRESSIVE* and see how when you were in the darkness, God has always been there, fulfilling His Word of never leaving nor abandoning you.

THE WILDERNESS PERIOD

There is a war going on…a fight for your mind. In the midst of darkness and the desert, you and I have to walk and stand strong while we deal in the portals of the wilderness without giving up or giving in. *The heavens are at war* and *here on earth. Again, we are at war*. This war is out to destroy all we worked so hard to build. This war is out to kill all we have sacrificed to get. This war is to make sure your mind breaks so you'll end up in a mental home or psych ward. *Even the Bible says that off the lips of Jesus the devil comes ONLY to kill us, to destroy us, and to rob from us*. When you make it out of the wilderness period you will feel like a champion. *Victory is yours. Don't let the war get into you but you fight with all you have in the name of Christ*. No one can stop you but you. Father God is with you. He will NEVER EVER abandon you and leave you an illegitimate child. *Never*. Once you come out of the wilderness…trust me, you will thank your Father for breaking you in the wilderness. You will come out stronger than ever. Watch and see.

The Bible says that without Jesus, we can do nothing…

John 15:5 (NKJV)
I AM the Vine; you are the branches. He who abides in Me, and I in him, bears much fruit; for without Me you can do nothing.

There are Christian leaders in churches that feel they can do ministry by their own power, violating the passage you just read. There is a rude awakening coming for those who stay consumed with this kind of thinking. Why? Because living this way is always short-lived. I do not understand why we don't take history into account of those who have lived this way before, in which so many have ended up losing in a terrible way. One reason is the devil blinds them and the other reason is God gives them over to a reprobate mind. To be honest I don't want to put myself in any of these categories. The scriptures declare repetitively that we are to humble ourselves instead of the Lord doing it. I am sure you know what that means in one form or another. It hurts when God does it, so it is better we humble ourselves.

The hand of the Lord is so heavy that it'll break you or mold you. This would be for your good. God knows having no purpose reigning in your spirit is a terrible place. He does not want that for you. With over 10,000 promises, the Bible shows He is a covenant Father. These promises can take you higher in the Spirit above all that you can ever ask or think. Watch God in how He is going to use you. You will be so overwhelmed that you'll think you are not alive. Leaving you in awe and catching you by surprise is how He operates at times. He loves blessing His Children He can trust. *The key is trust.*

In conclusion, I say to you, Zion, that stand faithful no matter what, and you will see your dreams come true for you and your family. And remember, friend, we are family. We love you.

EPILOGUE

I AM BELIEVING GOD THE WORDS WRITTEN here have been a blessing to you in some way or another. I have written this book to help you recognize the power you have within you and in the word of God, to live a life free from any type of stronghold(s) and chains.

The same power that raised Jesus Christ from the dead is available to us now in order to help us with our problems, so when you feel weak and limited don't despair, He has you in the palm of His hand. Remember that God can and will deliver you as well as give you the strength you need to resist the enemy. Therefore, you will receive the ability to recognize the deceitful tools satan uses to keep you entangled in bondage.

Mrs. Lewis wants you to trust the Word of God, why? Because it's holy, trustworthy and unchangeable. Be inspired to launch your faith out into the deep so you can live happy, unabridged and free! God promises great blessings to His people with many of them requiring active participation. He will deliver us, show us goodness, supply our every need, listen when we talk to Him and redeem us in due season.

Nothing you can do in your life can alter how God feels about you. You being able to read this book God the Holy Spirit gave me displays a willingness in your heart that you want change. All the glory goes to our Father! So, guard your mind Beloved knowing that the Almighty prevails. He will never fail you nor lead you astray. You have come this far, and He will not leave you just like that. Be encouraged Reader there is greater and more in God. *Run after it with all of your heart. Be FREE from all types of bondage and chains.* In fact, can you hear the chains falling? YOU ARE FREE! And where the Spirit of the LORD is, who's within you is FREE indeed! I end this book with this,

Zion! Walk in your FREEDOM!

ACKNOWLEDGEMENTS

I BLESS GOD FOR MY WONDERFUL HUSBAND, *Shawn Lewis*, of 20 years who have stood by my side helping me with other business ventures and ideas. Encouraging me to write this book. As he would support me and remind me to always write the vision down and make it plain. I appreciate you, and I'm confident that you are my true soul mate for life, I will always love you.

To my wonderful mother, *Edith Atkinson*, a strong woman of God who raised me the same, teaching me at an early age that I could do anything I want in life. And whatever I chose to strive for the absolute best in whatever I did keeping in mind to always place God first. I love you my queen with all my heart and I appreciate every sacrifice you've made for your children. I'm so blessed to have you as my mother.

To my Eldest sister, *Alicia*; my prayer partner and friend. I appreciate you taking my midnight calls, thank you for always having my back and being there for me when I need you. You're the best eldest sister a girl can have. I emphasize 'eldest' because I acknowledge that there is a responsibility that comes with being the eldest which I believe is often unrecognized by many. I want you to know sis, you did an awesome job.

I bless God for my younger sister, *Sebrina*, who always has a way of making me laugh even when I am not in the mood. Inspiring me to keep the faith and trust God no matter what.

To my baby sister, *Jackquline*, I will never forget the times you would drop everything you were doing (including your music projects) to come to the state of Virginia to support me during the times my body was under attack. I remember you telling me nothing is more important to you than the good Lord and family. Thank you, baby sis, I love you.

To my brother, *Kerry*, I'm so thankful to have a brother like you. You're always there when I need you. Truly you are a man of many gifts and talents, I love you with all my heart. I'm blessed to have a brother like you.

To my sons, *Samuel* and *Joshua*, you guys are such a wonderful blessing. I'm so proud of you both for being obedient and respectful as well as hard-working; always eager to learn. What a blessing from the Lord to have sons like you. I love you both with all of my heart.

To my dad, Apostle *Robert Dunson*, I thank you for spiritual counseling and helping me to clarify with good understanding about the word of God. Thank you for interceding for me and encouraging me to keep the faith, I love you.

Acknowledgements

To my mother-in-law, *Lillian Stewart*, who received me with open arms and often reminds me that I'm a blessing. I want you to know you are a blessing to me and I love you.

To my uncle, *Jimmy,* I say words cannot express how much I appreciate you. You have supported me on so many levels throughout the years. You have been more than an uncle to me, more like a father figure. I wanted to take this moment and honor you for your willingness. I love you so much.

To my aunt, *Wanda*, I have a ton of great memories that I often say with a smile on your teaching us how to do the hustle, making sweet cornbread, and applying my first lipstick. I have to say you were the best baby sitter/auntie a girl could have. I'll hold on to those sweet memories. I love you so much.

To my uncle, *Jackie* thank you for teaching me to speak up for myself so that no one can push me around. Thank you for the wild rides on the back of your motorcycle I can still hear you yelling for me to lean with you through the curves and to hold on tight! Thank you for the fun times.

To the rest of my family Aunt *Melissa*, my cousins and my best friend since first grade *Angelia Paige*. I love and appreciate you and thank you for supporting me through it all.

ABOUT THE AUTHOR

*D*EMECIA LEWIS WAS BORN AND RAISED IN Roanoke, Alabama. She graduated from Handley High School. Demecia furthered her education at Philips Jr. College in Columbus, Georgia and West Georgia Technical Institute in LaGrange, Georgia, where she majored in business administration.

Demecia Lewis is co-owner of S&J Lewis Consulting Solutions. She is also the owner of *"Dee's Lovely Things"* a wholesale company of home decorations and clothing. She is the founder of a charitable organization called "Hearts of Love".

Demecia married retired Gunnery Sergeant Shawn Lewis in 1997 and moved to Okinawa Japan where their 1st born son, Samuel was born. Several years later, in 2002, they had their second son Joshua, while residing in Rockmart, Georgia.

Demecia has overcome many obstacles in life after being diagnosed with MS (multiple sclerosis). Ever since her personal relationship with the Lord Jesus including the support of her family, she made a declaration of faith. I questioned myself within. Whose report will I receive? I believe the report of the Lord. By faith she received her healing as she continues to walk by faith, encourage, and intercede for others. Saved at the age of 12 years old she declares that nothing will ever separate her from her Lord and Savior Jesus.

Appendix A

PRAYER OF SALVATION

FATHER, I AM A SINNER, AND I ASK YOU TO forgive me of my sins. Cleanse me with Your blood and wash me from all unrighteousness. I believe that Jesus died on the cross for my sins, and on the third day, you raised Him from the dead. Father, I ask You to fill me with Your Holy Spirit now and write my name in the Lamb's Book of Life. I give my entire life to You from this day on. In Jesus' name, I pray, Amen.

If you confess with your mouth the Lord Jesus and believe in your heart that God has raised Him from the dead, you will be saved. For with the heart one believes unto righteousness, and with the mouth confession is made unto salvation. (Romans 10:9-10 NKJV).

BAPTISM OF THE HOLY SPIRIT

Heavenly Father, I plead the Blood of my Lord and Savior Jesus Christ over me and I thank You for the most wonderful gift of salvation. Lord Jesus You promised me another gift, the gift of the Holy Spirit. So, I ask You Lord Jesus, to baptize and fill me in and with Your Holy Spirit, just as You filled Your disciples on the day of Pentecost. Christ Jesus, I am one of your disciple(s), filled with the Holy Spirit just as Your disciples. I will try to do what You tell me to do, I forgive all those who have ever caused me pain, trauma, shock, harm, rejection, or shame, and I ask You to forgive them. I also ask You to forgive me for holding a judgement against them.

Thank You Lord Jesus that I am filled with Your Holy Spirit and begin to speak with other tongues, as the Spirit gives me utterance. *(Acts 2:4 KJV).*

CONTACT INFO

For booking or Speaking Engagements:

DEMECIA LEWIS

Email:
demecia_lewis@hotmail.com

God is Sovereign
And
He Makes all things
new. May He Continue
to bless & keep you

Dununc Lewis

To: N.D.

May God Bless
You!